Disney
THE LION KING

MUSIC FROM THE MOTION PICTURE SOUNDTRACK

ISBN 978-1-5400-6755-5

Motion Picture Artwork TM & Copyright © 2019 Disney

Visit Hal Leonard Online at
www.halleonard.com

Contact us:
Hal Leonard
7777 West Bluemound Road
Milwaukee, WI 53213
Email: info@halleonard.com

In Europe, contact:
Hal Leonard Europe Limited
42 Wigmore Street
Marylebone, London, W1U 2RN
Email: info@halleonardeurope.com

In Australia, contact:
Hal Leonard Australia Pty. Ltd.
4 Lentara Court
Cheltenham, Victoria, 3192 Australia
Email: info@halleonard.com.au

CIRCLE OF LIFE/NANTS' INGONYAMA

NANTS' INGONYAMA
Music and Lyrics by LEBOHANG MORAKE
and HANS ZIMMER

Moderately, with an African beat

Same tempo, gently rhythmic

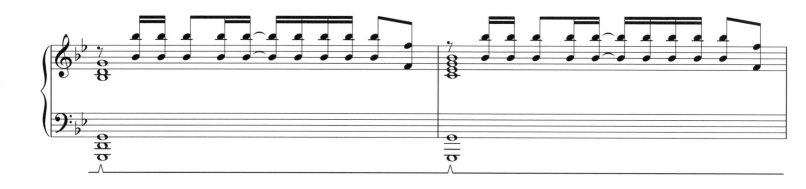

CIRCLE OF LIFE
Music by ELTON JOHN
Lyrics by TIM RICE

(With pedal)

8vb -

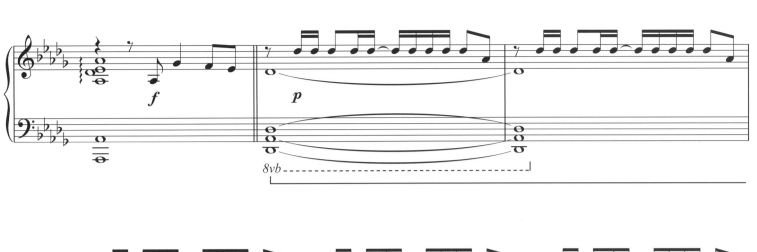

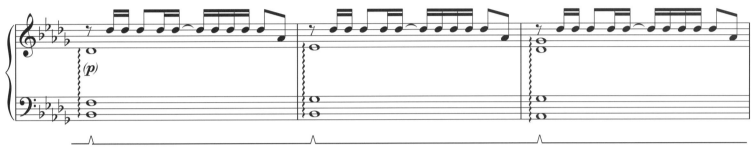

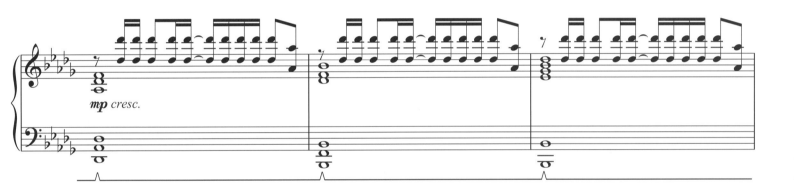

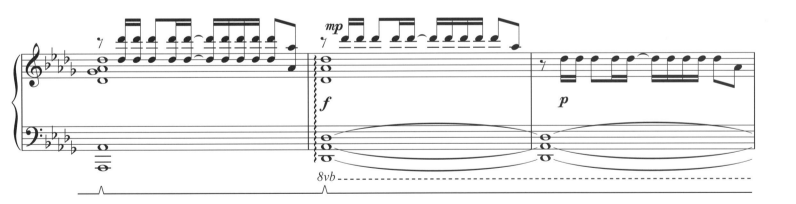

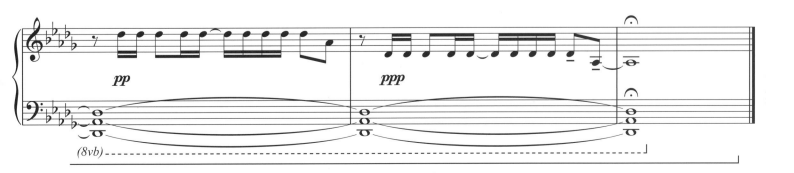

RAFIKI'S FIREFLIES

Composed by
HANS ZIMMER

I JUST CAN'T WAIT TO BE KING

Music by ELTON JOHN
Lyrics by TIM RICE

Happily, rhythmically

SCAR TAKES THE THRONE

Composed by
HANS ZIMMER

Moderately

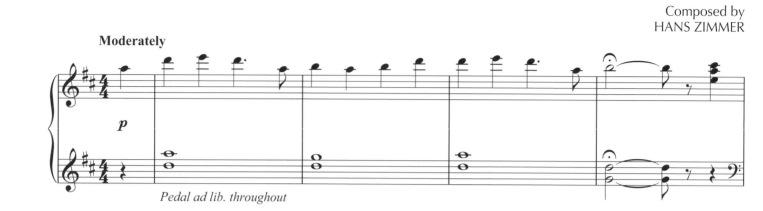

Pedal ad lib. throughout

Slowly, expressively

HAKUNA MATATA

Music by ELTON JOHN
Lyrics by TIM RICE

Freely, with soul

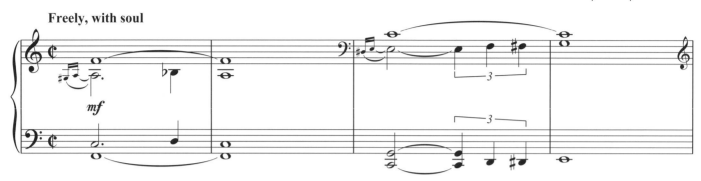

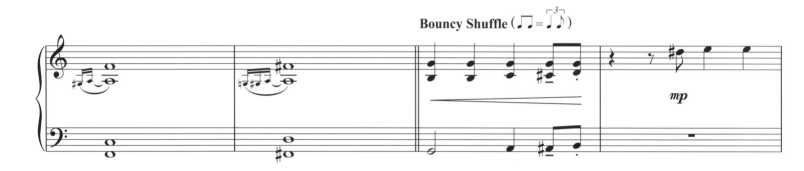

With operatic flair (♫ = ♫)

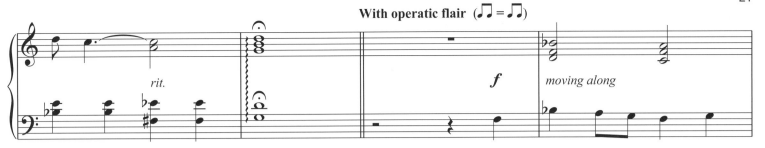

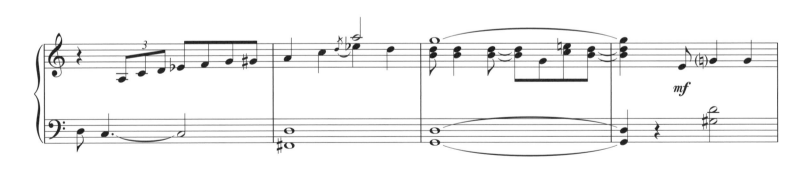

SIMBA IS ALIVE!

Composed by
HANS ZIMMER

Moderately slow

mp

Pedal ad lib. throughout

rit.

CAN YOU FEEL THE LOVE TONIGHT

Music by ELTON JOHN
Lyrics by TIM RICE

SPIRIT

Written by TIMOTHY McKENZIE,
ILYA SALMANZADEH and BEYONCÉ

32

BATTLE FOR PRIDE ROCK

Composed by
HANS ZIMMER

Moderately slow, expressively

Moderately

REMEMBER

Composed by HANS ZIMMER
"Circle of Life" Music by ELTON JOHN
Lyrics by TIM RICE

Half as fast ($\quarternote = \eighthnote$)

NEVER TOO LATE

Music by ELTON JOHN
Lyrics by TIM RICE